Veronica Engel

Floral Sea

A Coloring Book Underwater Adventure

SEA STALLION
PUBLICATIONS

SeaStallionPublications.com
P.O. Box 6756
San Diego, CA 92106

Copyright©2018 By Veronica Engel

Designed By Veronica Engel
Printed in the United States Of America

www.AdultColoringBooksByVeronica.com

This book belongs to

....

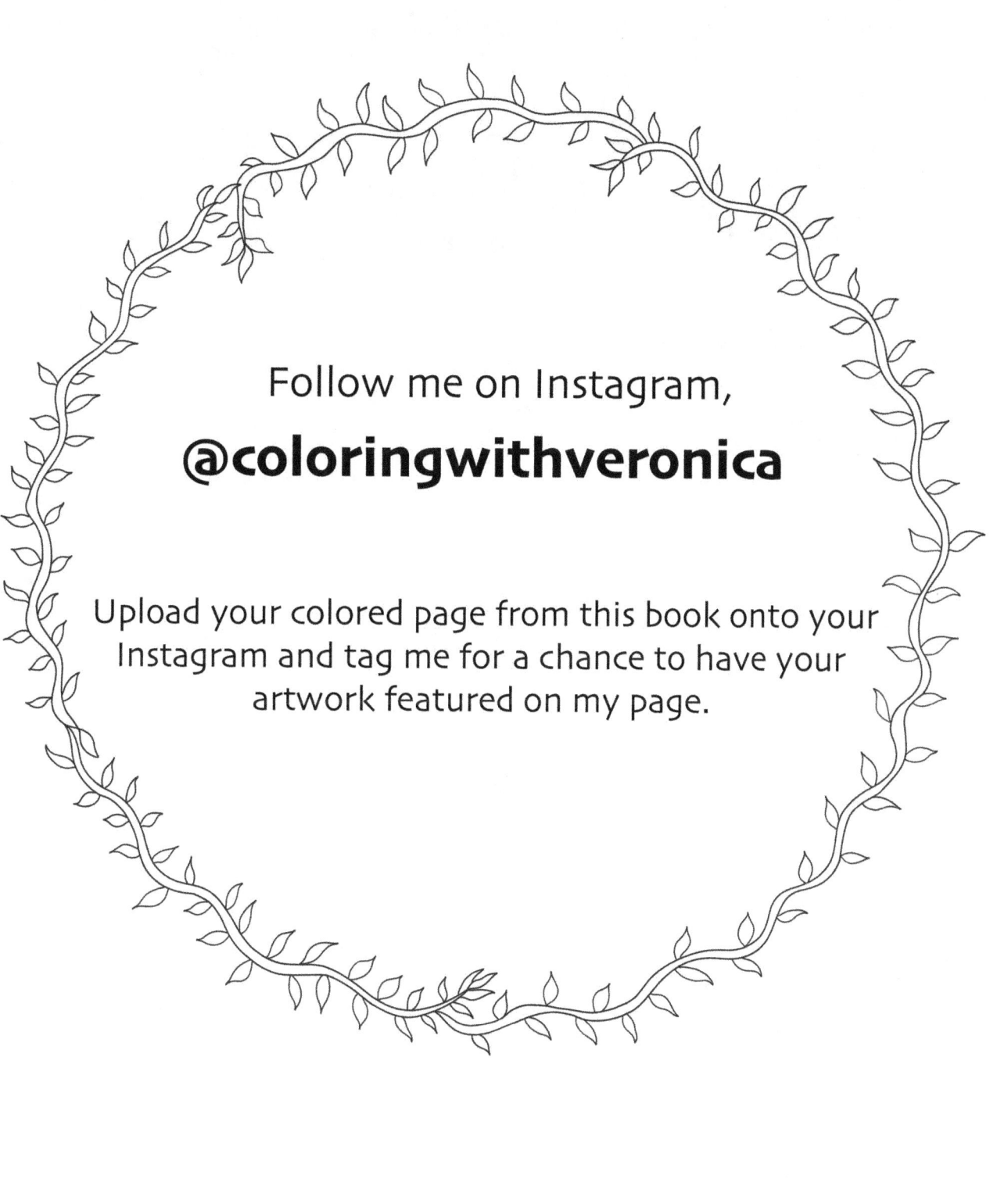

Follow me on Instagram,

@coloringwithveronica

Upload your colored page from this book onto your Instagram and tag me for a chance to have your artwork featured on my page.

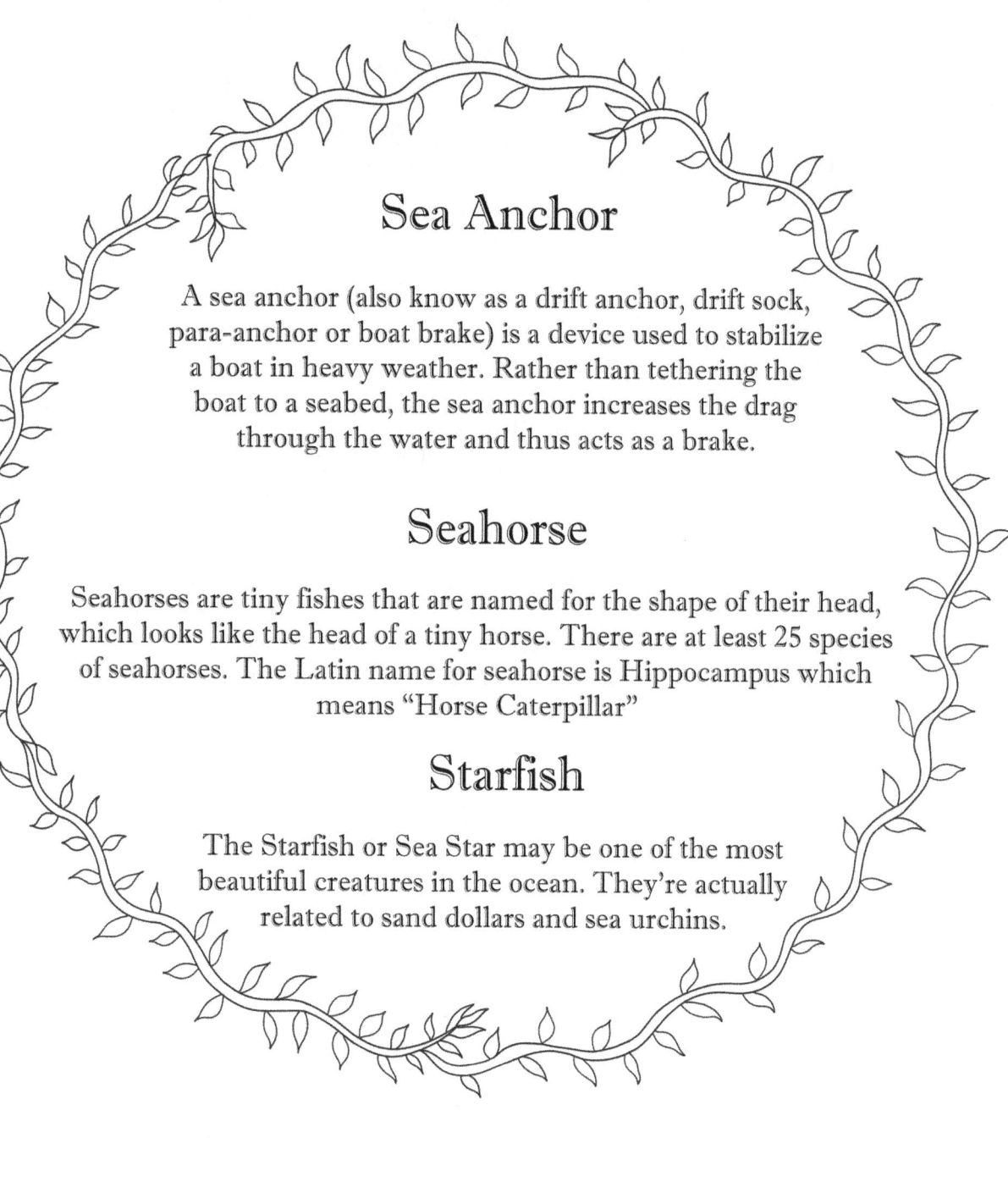

Sea Anchor

A sea anchor (also know as a drift anchor, drift sock, para-anchor or boat brake) is a device used to stabilize a boat in heavy weather. Rather than tethering the boat to a seabed, the sea anchor increases the drag through the water and thus acts as a brake.

Seahorse

Seahorses are tiny fishes that are named for the shape of their head, which looks like the head of a tiny horse. There are at least 25 species of seahorses. The Latin name for seahorse is Hippocampus which means "Horse Caterpillar"

Starfish

The Starfish or Sea Star may be one of the most beautiful creatures in the ocean. They're actually related to sand dollars and sea urchins.

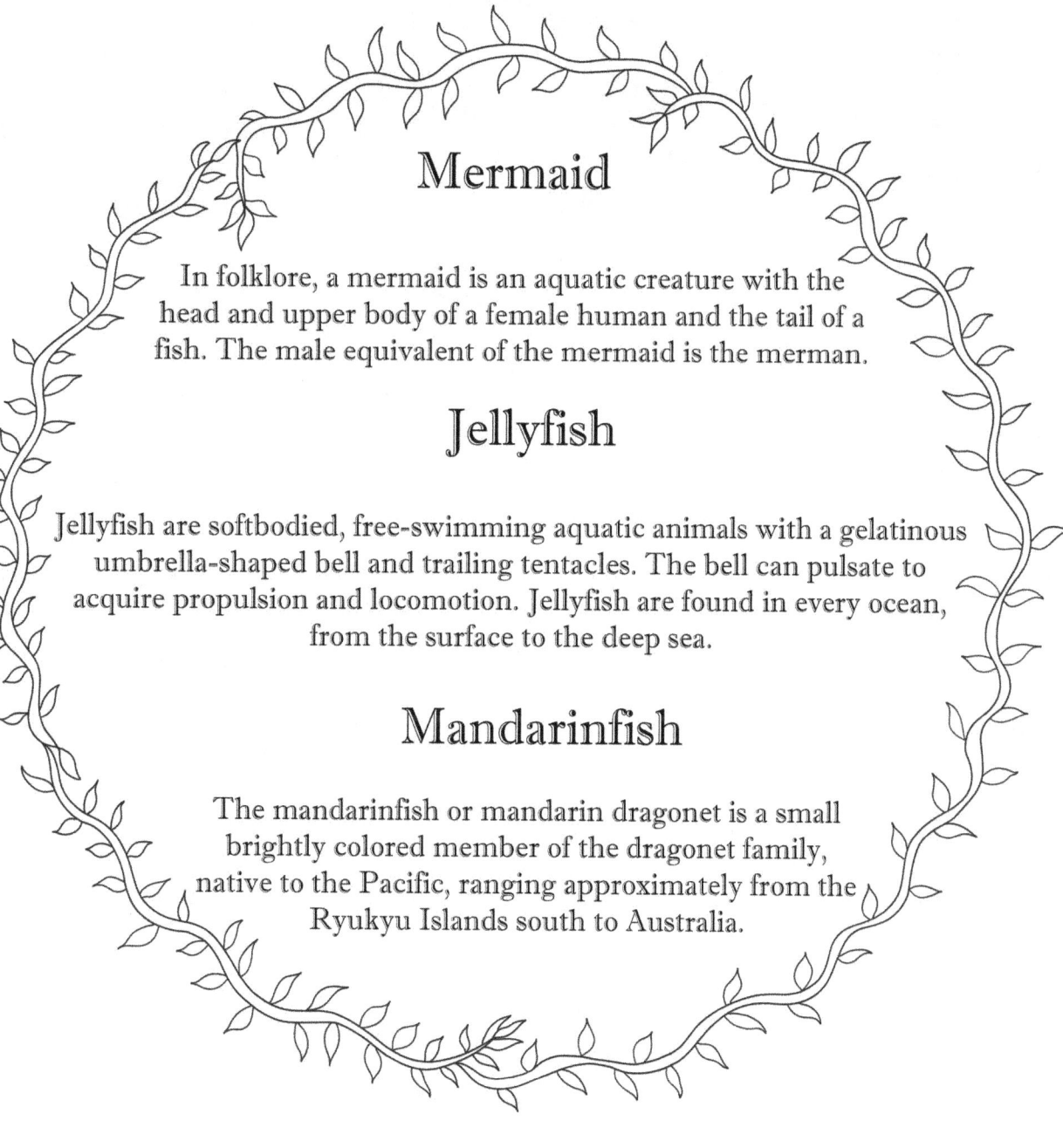

Mermaid

In folklore, a mermaid is an aquatic creature with the head and upper body of a female human and the tail of a fish. The male equivalent of the mermaid is the merman.

Jellyfish

Jellyfish are softbodied, free-swimming aquatic animals with a gelatinous umbrella-shaped bell and trailing tentacles. The bell can pulsate to acquire propulsion and locomotion. Jellyfish are found in every ocean, from the surface to the deep sea.

Mandarinfish

The mandarinfish or mandarin dragonet is a small brightly colored member of the dragonet family, native to the Pacific, ranging approximately from the Ryukyu Islands south to Australia.

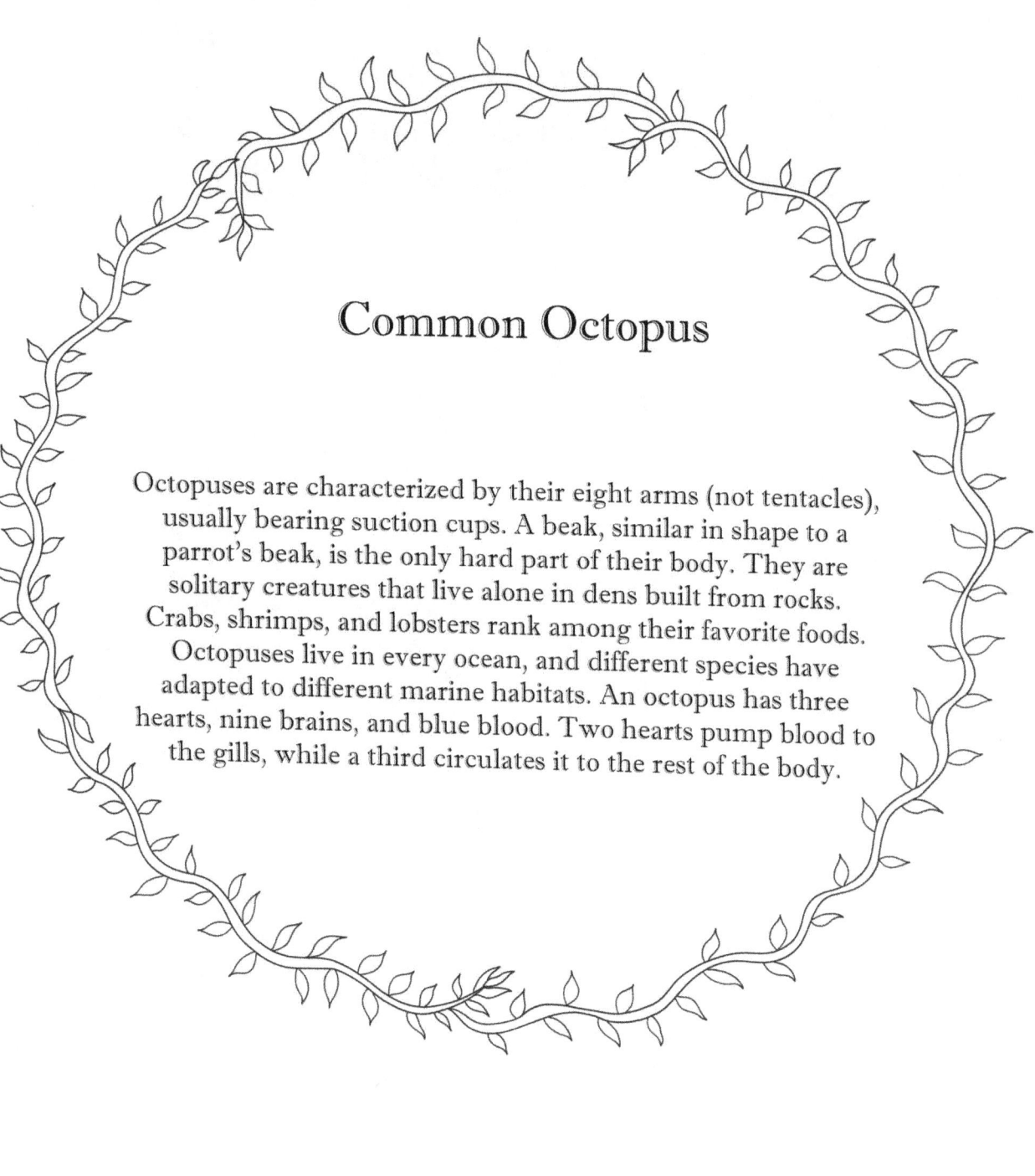

Common Octopus

Octopuses are characterized by their eight arms (not tentacles), usually bearing suction cups. A beak, similar in shape to a parrot's beak, is the only hard part of their body. They are solitary creatures that live alone in dens built from rocks. Crabs, shrimps, and lobsters rank among their favorite foods. Octopuses live in every ocean, and different species have adapted to different marine habitats. An octopus has three hearts, nine brains, and blue blood. Two hearts pump blood to the gills, while a third circulates it to the rest of the body.

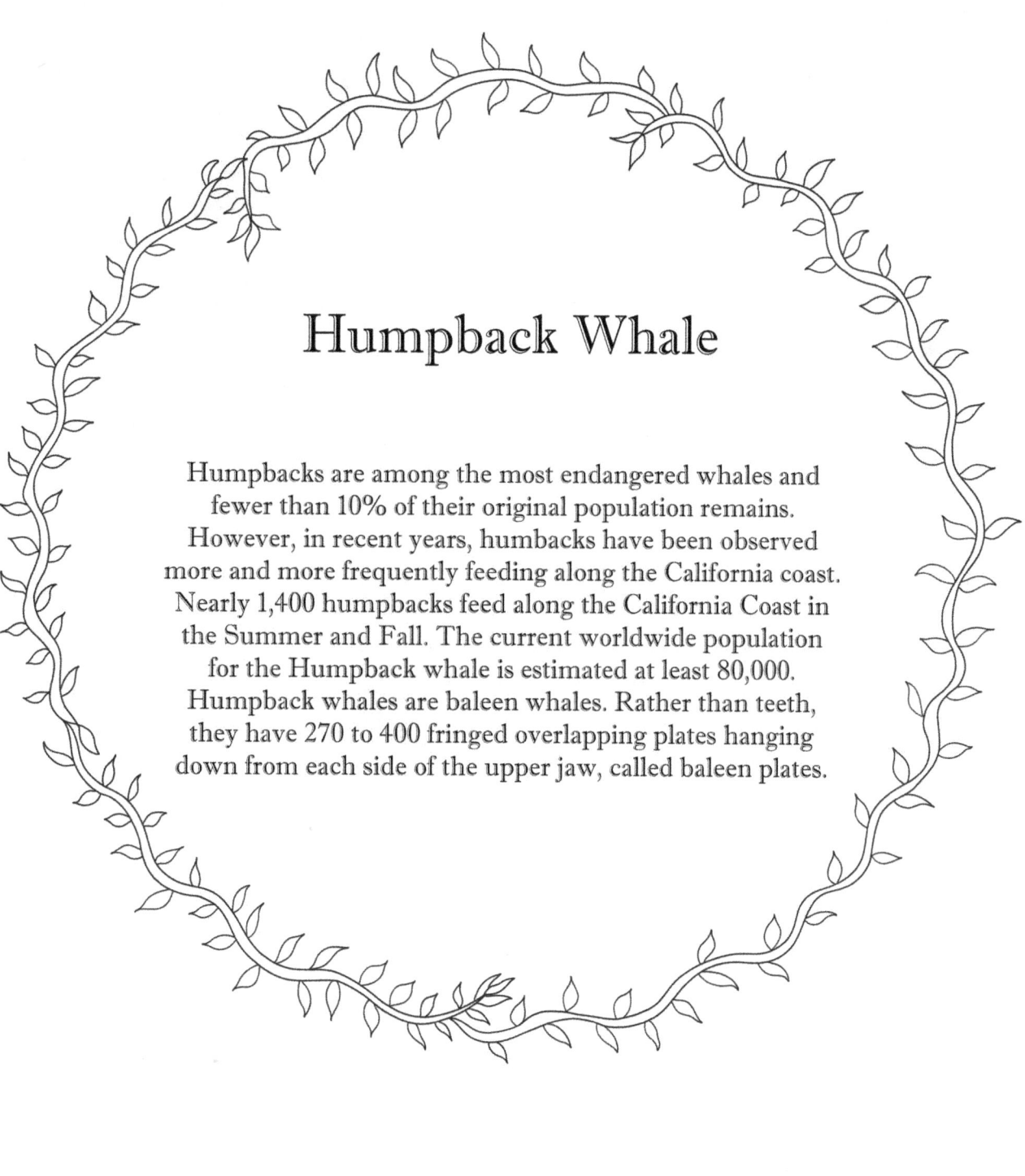

Humpback Whale

Humpbacks are among the most endangered whales and fewer than 10% of their original population remains. However, in recent years, humbacks have been observed more and more frequently feeding along the California coast. Nearly 1,400 humpbacks feed along the California Coast in the Summer and Fall. The current worldwide population for the Humpback whale is estimated at least 80,000. Humpback whales are baleen whales. Rather than teeth, they have 270 to 400 fringed overlapping plates hanging down from each side of the upper jaw, called baleen plates.

Starfish

Starfish or sea stars are star-shaped echinoderms belonging to the class Asteroidea. Starfish are marine invertebrates. Most can regenerate damaged parts or lost arms and they can shed arms as a means of defense. The starfish are a large and diverse class with about 2,000 living species from every ocean basin in the world, including the Atlantic, Indian, and Pacific as well as the Artic and the Southern Ocean.

Sea Turtle

Sea turtles are one of the Earth's most ancient creatures. The seven species that can be found today have been around for 110 million years, since the time of dinosaurs. Nearly all species of sea turtle are classified as Endangered. The sea turtle's shell, or "carapace" is streamlined for swimming through the water. Unlike other turtles, sea turtles cannot retract their legs and head into their shells. Sea turtles, like salmon, will return to the same nesting grounds at which they were born.

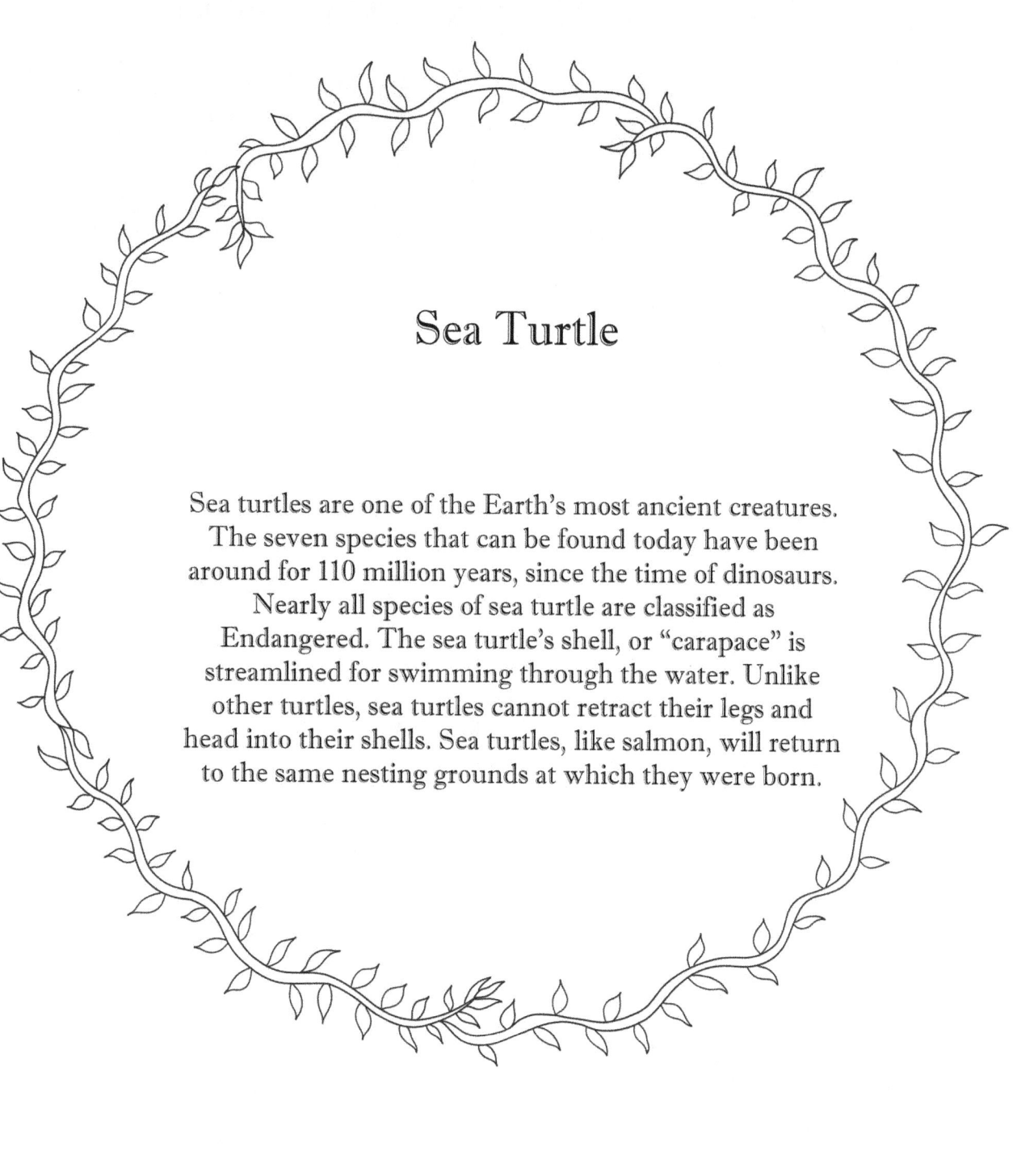

King Helmet Conch Shell

The King Helmet scientific name Cassis Turberosa is the largest of the Carribbean Helmet shells. Mature Kings are identified by their triangular base. Helmets are found in shallow, tropical waters.

Starfish

Starfish are marine intertebrates. They typically have a central disc and five arms, though some species have a larger number of arms.

Auger Shell

The shells of the sea snails in this family are typically shaped like slender augers or screws. In that respect they share certain shell characters with the family Turritellidae, the turret shells.

Maine Lobster

Maine lobsters are clawed lobsters, and have large, meaty claws. Spiny Caribbean lobsters have no claws and are sold mainly for their tails. Lobsters are invertebrate members of the Class Crustacea of the Phylum Arthropoda. Lobsters usually feed on bottom dwellers like clams, snails, and crabs. Lobsters can live to over 100 years old.

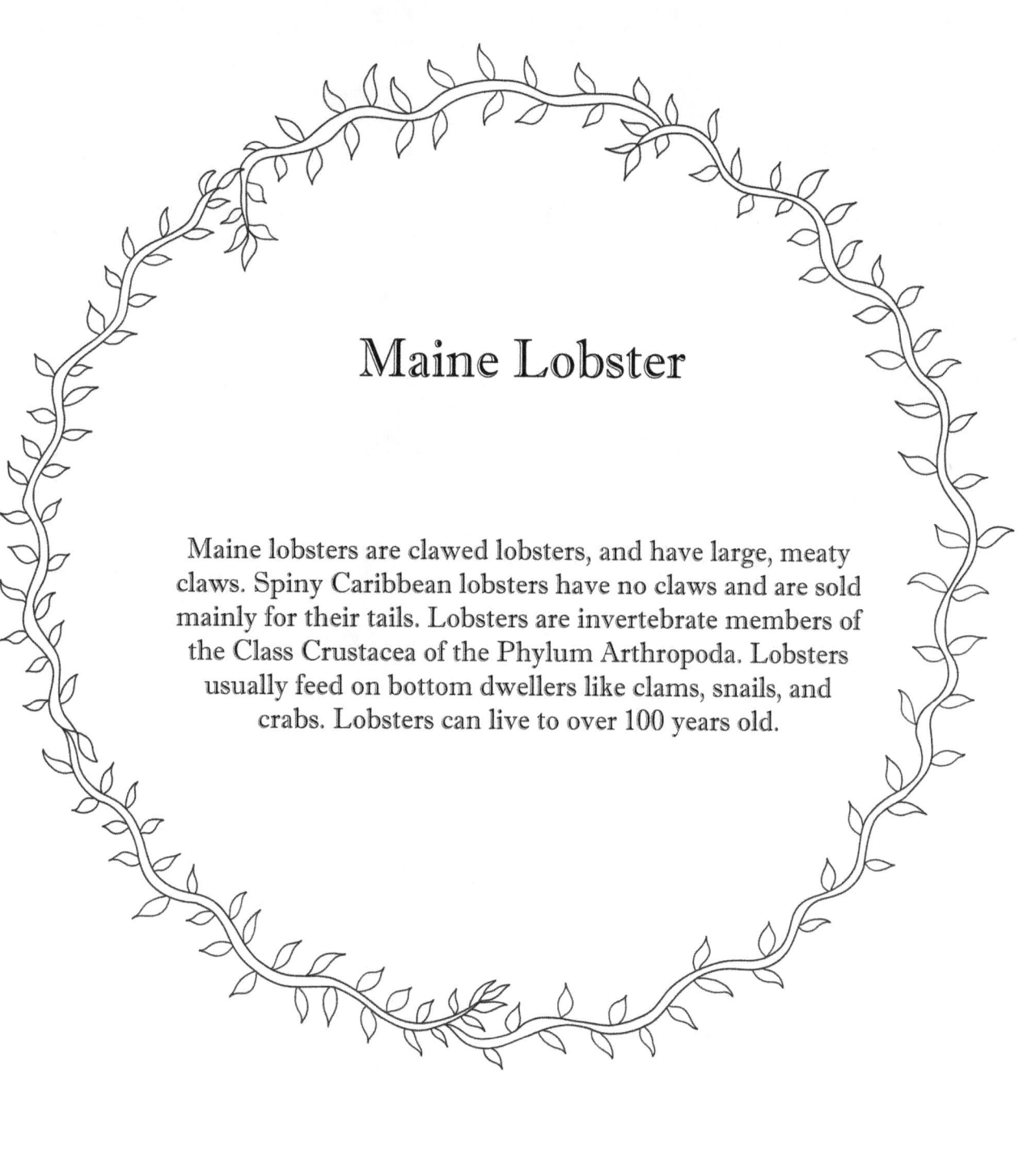

Broadbill Swordfish

The broadbill, or Xiphias gladius, which is found in tropical, temperate and sometimes even cold waters in the Atlantic, Pacific and Indian oceans, is a powerful, agressive and majestic-looking creature, and is perhaps the ultimate quarry in fishing. It's the true gladiator of the deep. Swordfish is a particularly popular fish for cooking. Since swordfish are large animals, meat is usually sold as steaks, which are often grilled. Swordfish meat is relatively firm and can be cooked in ways more fragile types of fish cannot (such as over a grill on skewers)

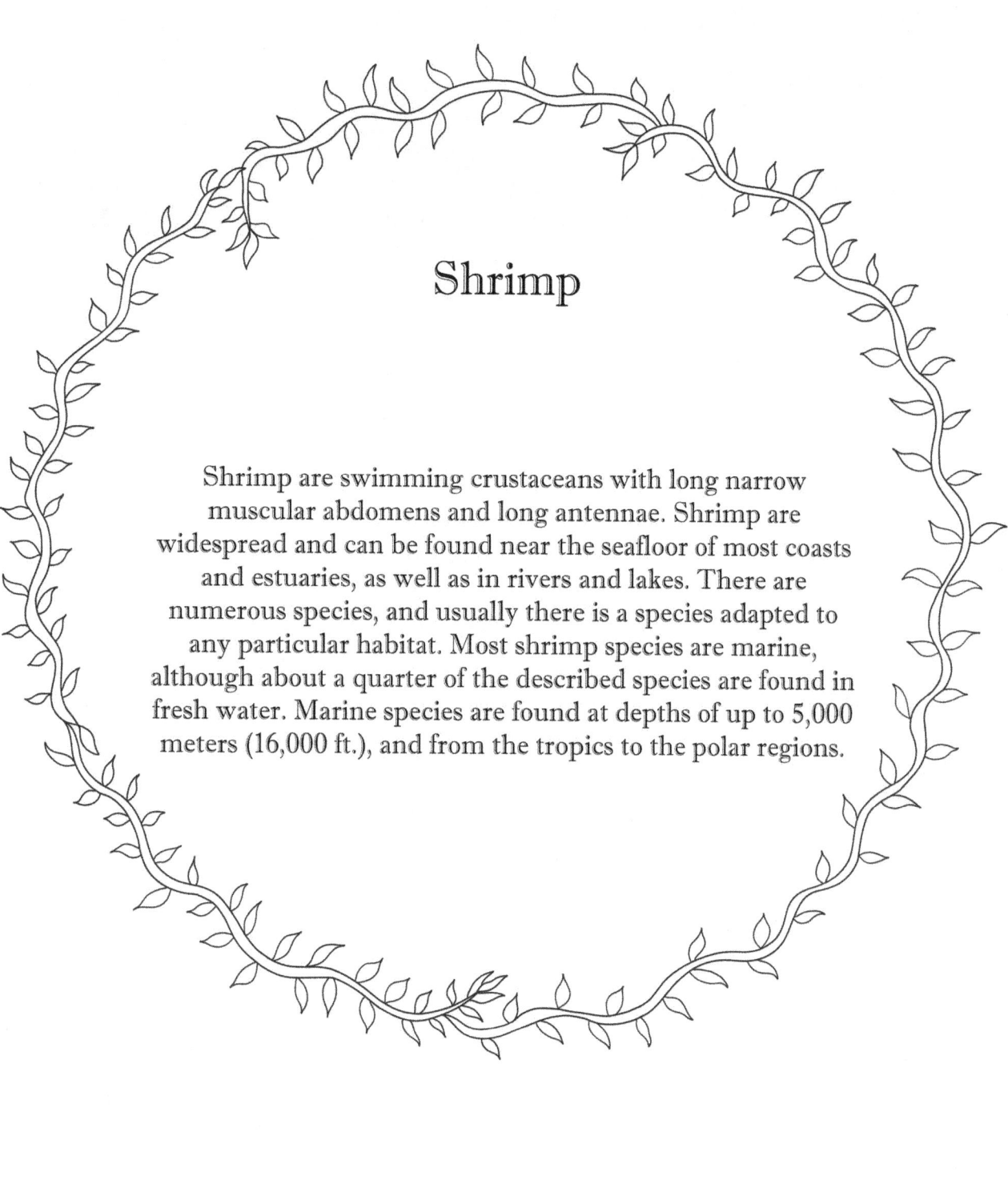

Shrimp

Shrimp are swimming crustaceans with long narrow muscular abdomens and long antennae. Shrimp are widespread and can be found near the seafloor of most coasts and estuaries, as well as in rivers and lakes. There are numerous species, and usually there is a species adapted to any particular habitat. Most shrimp species are marine, although about a quarter of the described species are found in fresh water. Marine species are found at depths of up to 5,000 meters (16,000 ft.), and from the tropics to the polar regions.

Chambered Nautilus

The chambered natutilus, Nautilus pompilius, also called the pearly nautilus, is the best-know species of nautilus. The chambered nautilus is both an active predator and scavenger. The chambered nautilus is one of the longest living cephalopods, reaching ages of over 20 years old. The nautilus are also the only cephalopods that reproduce multiple times. Squids, octopuses, and other cephalopods die after they reproduce once.

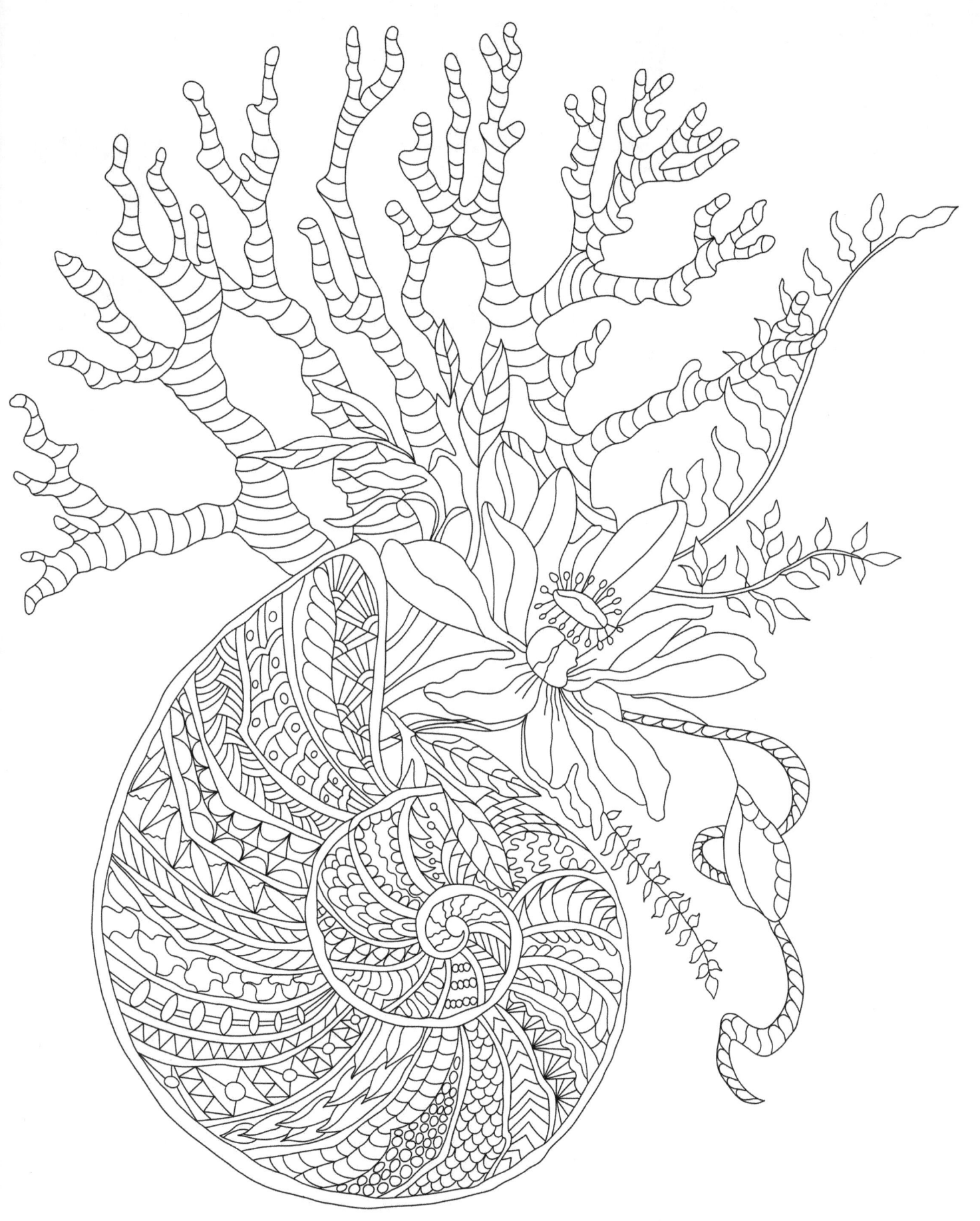

Dolphin

Dolphins are highly intelligent marine mammals and are part of the family of toothed whales that includes orcas and pilot whales. Nearly 40 species of dolphins swim the waters of the world. They live in social groups of five to several hundred are found worldwide, mostly in shallow seas of the continental shelves, and are carnivores, mostly eating fish and squid.

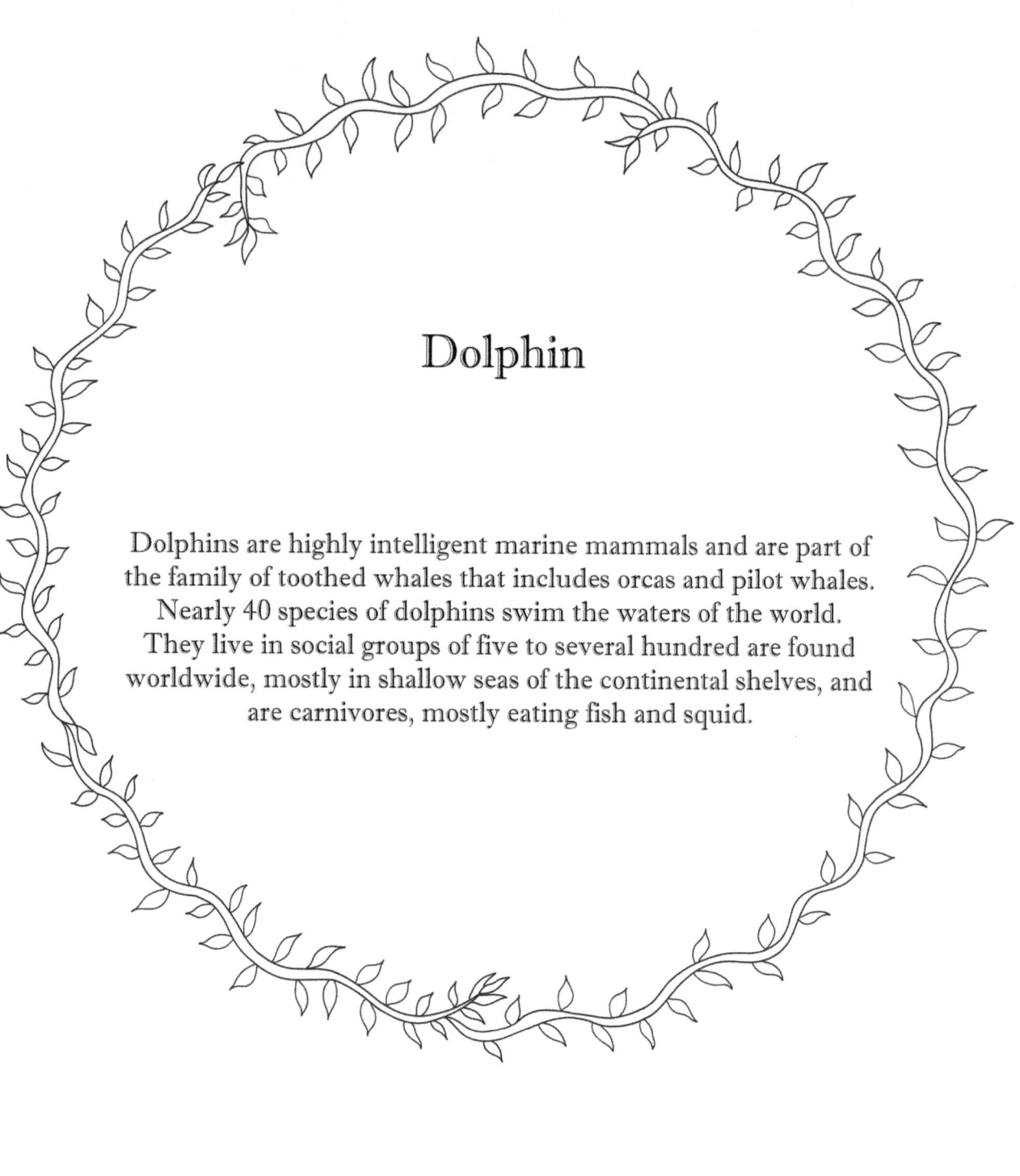

Dolphin

Dolphins are highly intelligent marine
mammals who live in social groups.
Dolphins are fast, active swimmers with
sharp, conical-pointed teeth for grasping
smooth-skinned, shallow-water fish and squid.
Dolphin communities survive eating fish and squid.

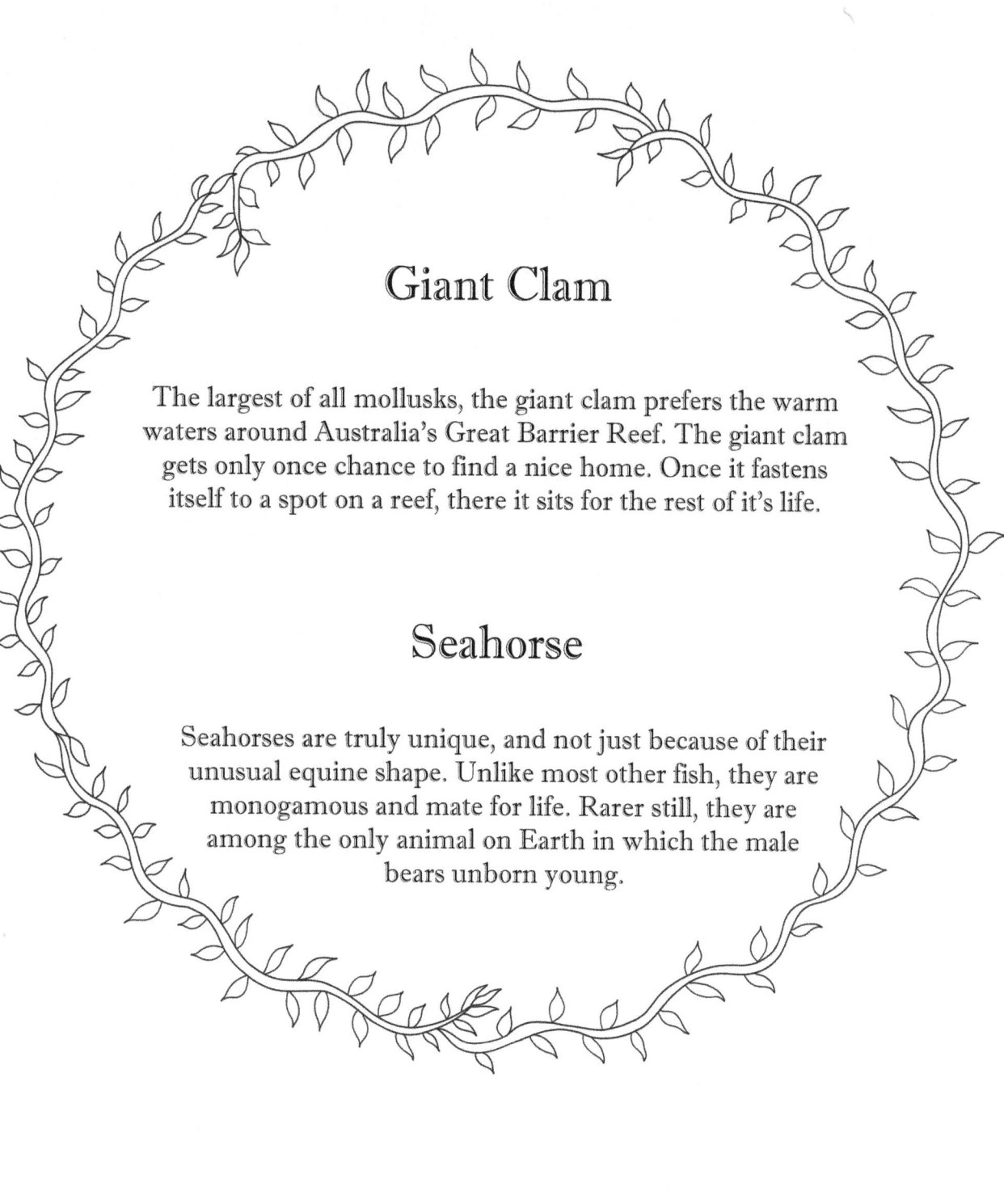

Giant Clam

The largest of all mollusks, the giant clam prefers the warm waters around Australia's Great Barrier Reef. The giant clam gets only once chance to find a nice home. Once it fastens itself to a spot on a reef, there it sits for the rest of it's life.

Seahorse

Seahorses are truly unique, and not just because of their unusual equine shape. Unlike most other fish, they are monogamous and mate for life. Rarer still, they are among the only animal on Earth in which the male bears unborn young.

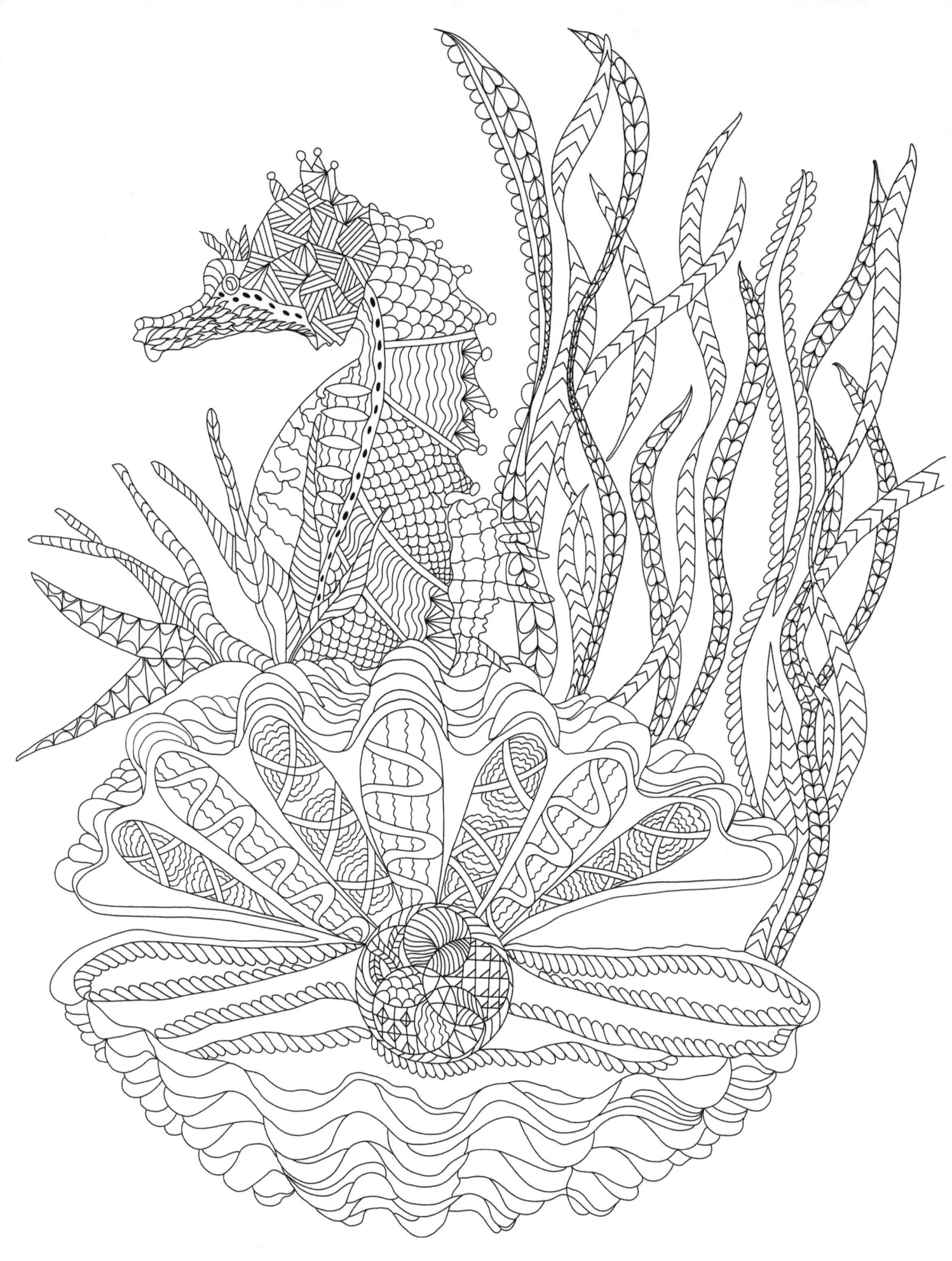

Cockle Shells

A cockle is a small, edible saltwater clam, a marine bivalve mollusk. True cockles live in sandy, sheltered beaches throughout the world. There are more than 200 different species of cockle throughout the world.

Turritella Seashells

Turritella seashells are also know as "screw shells". They have slender spirals and range in color from tan to dark brown. They can be found on sandy mud in the S.W. Pacific.

Sand Dollar

Sand dollars are of the Phylum Echinodermata, class Echinoidea. They, like the sea urchin, have no arms or legs but move around by tiny spines on there body. Sand dollars live on on sandy or muddy flat areas of the ocean floor in shallow water near land.

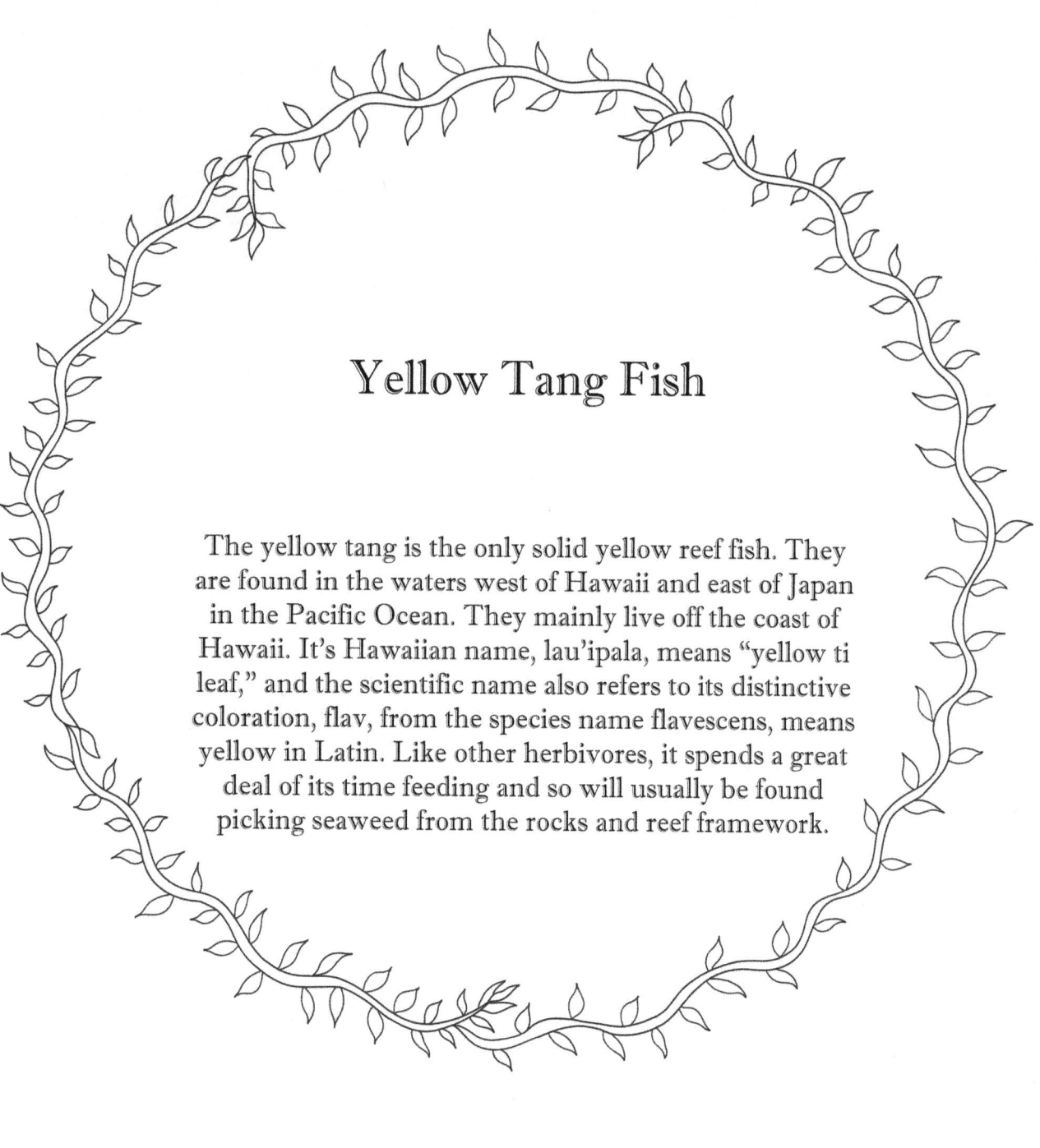

Yellow Tang Fish

The yellow tang is the only solid yellow reef fish. They are found in the waters west of Hawaii and east of Japan in the Pacific Ocean. They mainly live off the coast of Hawaii. It's Hawaiian name, lau'ipala, means "yellow ti leaf," and the scientific name also refers to its distinctive coloration, flav, from the species name flavescens, means yellow in Latin. Like other herbivores, it spends a great deal of its time feeding and so will usually be found picking seaweed from the rocks and reef framework.

Atlantic Triton's Trumpet Shell

The common name "Triton's Trumpet" is derived from the Greek god Triton, who was the son of Poseidon, god of the sea. It prefers to eat other snails and sea stars, most notably the Crown-of-thorns starfish, which feed on reef-building corals, are know to threaten the health of coral reefs. The giant triton is one of the only natural predators of that starfish. For that reason, this species is considered by the Australian government to be extremely important to reef health and is given legal protection in that country and others.

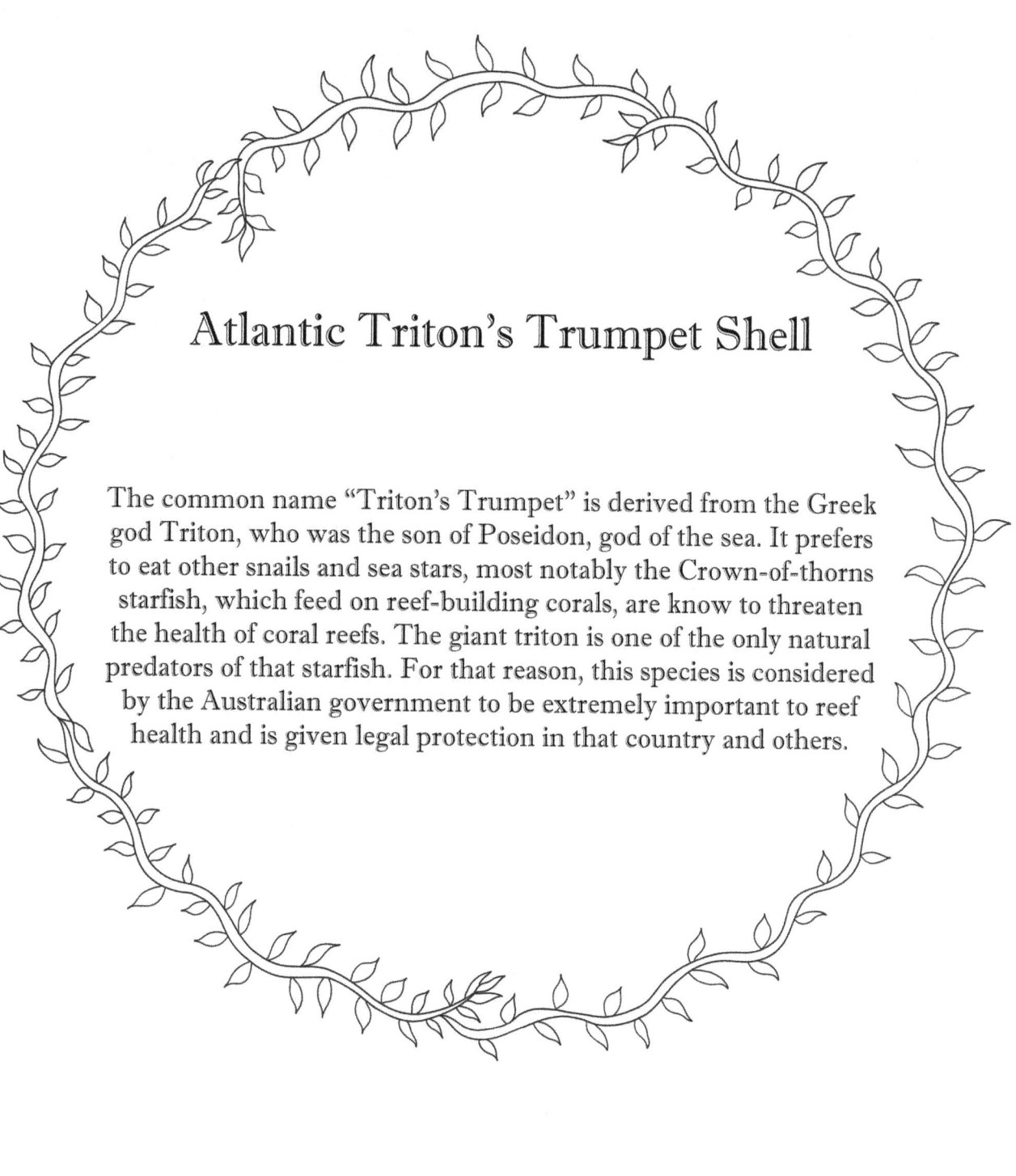

Queen Angelfish

The queen angelfish is one of the most iconic, brightly colored species on coral reefs of the Caribbean Sea and its adjacent waters. It is typically bright yellow, green, and blue, and it gets its name from the coloration on its head that gives the impression that it is wearing a crown. This species' thin, disc-shaped body makes it difficult to see head on but very easy to see from the side.

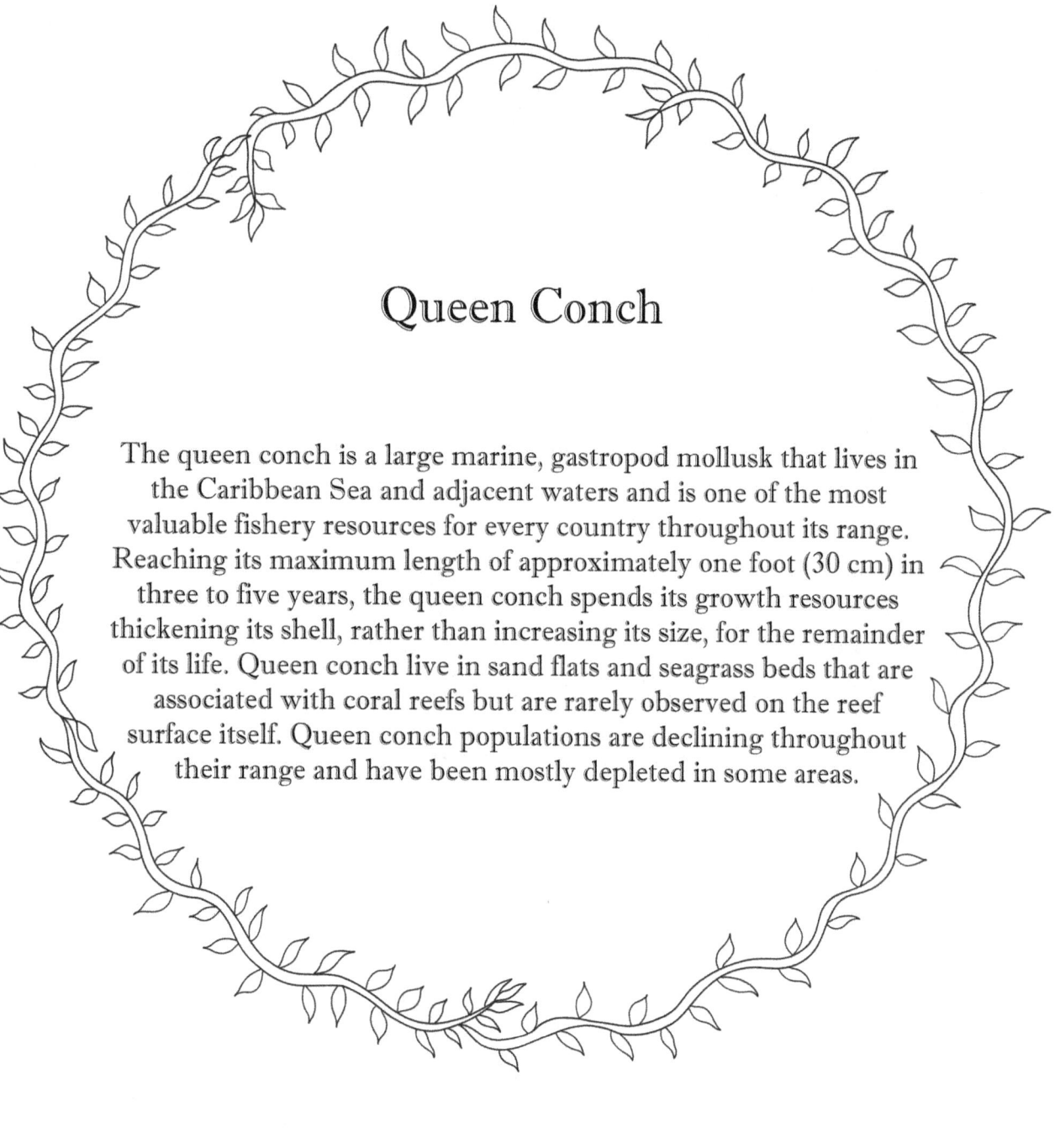

Queen Conch

The queen conch is a large marine, gastropod mollusk that lives in the Caribbean Sea and adjacent waters and is one of the most valuable fishery resources for every country throughout its range. Reaching its maximum length of approximately one foot (30 cm) in three to five years, the queen conch spends its growth resources thickening its shell, rather than increasing its size, for the remainder of its life. Queen conch live in sand flats and seagrass beds that are associated with coral reefs but are rarely observed on the reef surface itself. Queen conch populations are declining throughout their range and have been mostly depleted in some areas.

Lion's Paw Half Scallop Shell

Scallops are a cosmopolitan family of bivalves which are found in all of the world's oceans, with the largest number of species living in the Indo-Pacific region. Many species of scallop are highly prized as a food source, and some are farmed as aquaculture.

Eel

Eels are some of the more interesting creatures of the sea, with about 800 marine eel species known to science. Most eels live in the shallow waters of the ocean and burrow into sand, mud, or amongst rocks. A majority of eel species are nocturnal, thus are rarely seen. Sometimes, they are seen living together in holes of "eel pits". Some species of eels also live in deeper water on the continental shelves and over the slopes deep as 4,000 m (13,000 ft.).

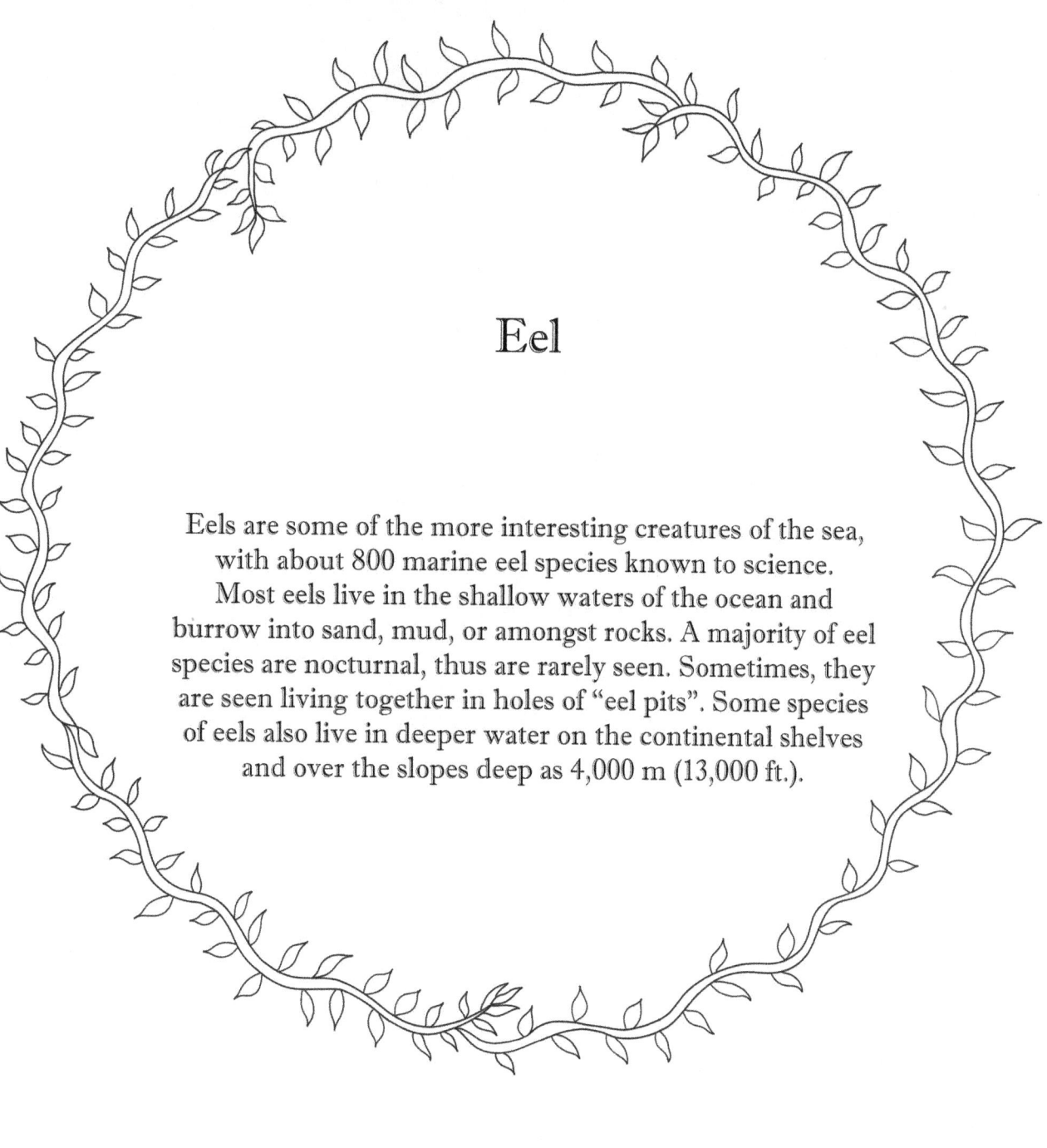

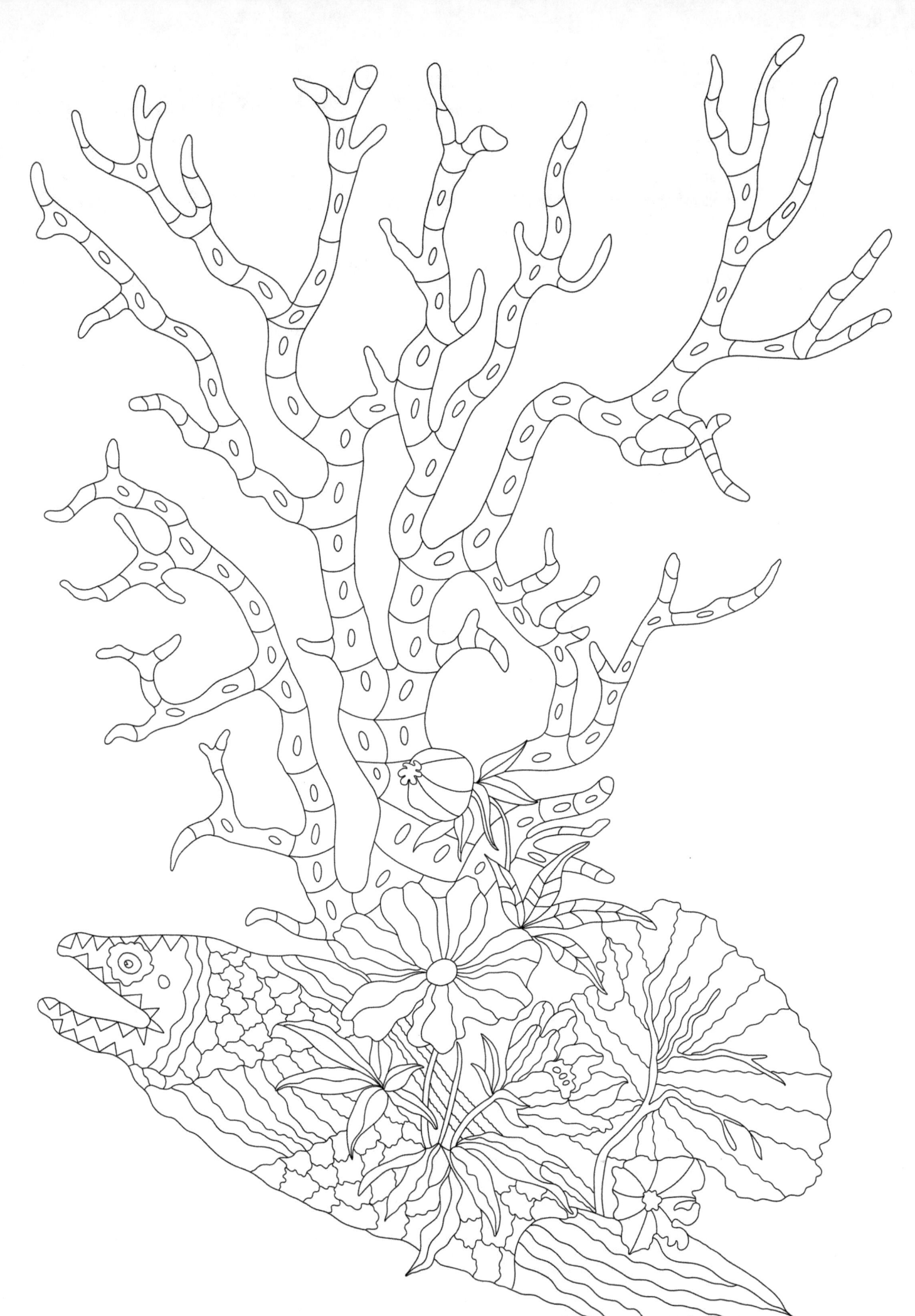

Red Lionfish

The red lionfish is a venomous coral reef fish found in the Indo-Pacific region, but has become an invasive problem in the Caribbean Sea, as well as along the East Coast of the United States. It has large venomous spines that protrude from the body similar to a mane, giving it the common name lionfish. They can be found around the seaward edge of reefs and coral, in lagoons, and on rocky surfaces. The average red lionfish lives around 10 years.

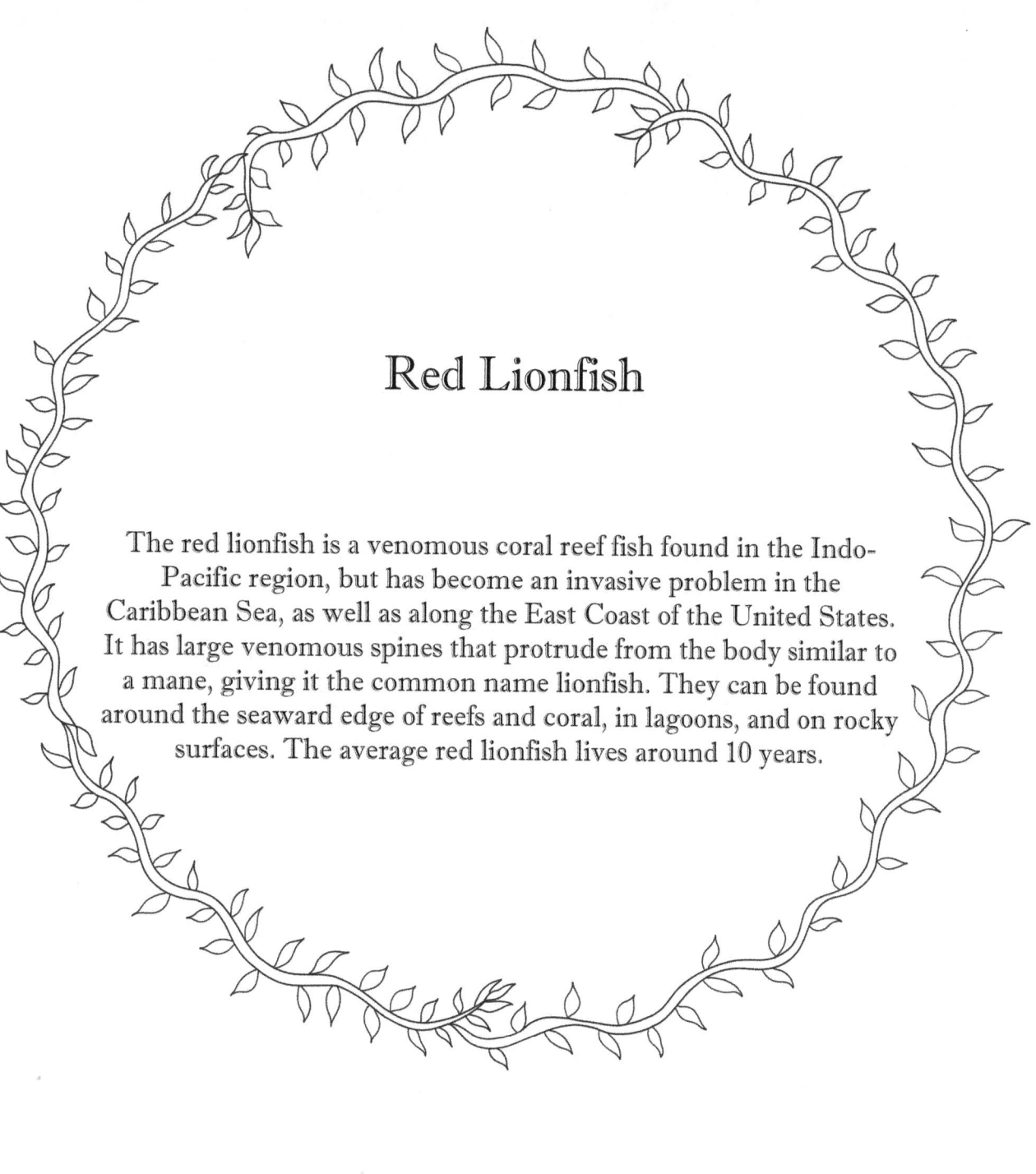

Clownfish

Clownfish live in the venomous tentacles of sea anemones. They are one of the only ocean creatures that can do this as they are protected by a layer of slimy mucus on their skin. Clownfish like to live in sea anemones so that they are protected from predators and can nibble on leftover food the sea anemone catches. in return, they help keep sea anemones and the area clean by eating up algae and other reef debris.

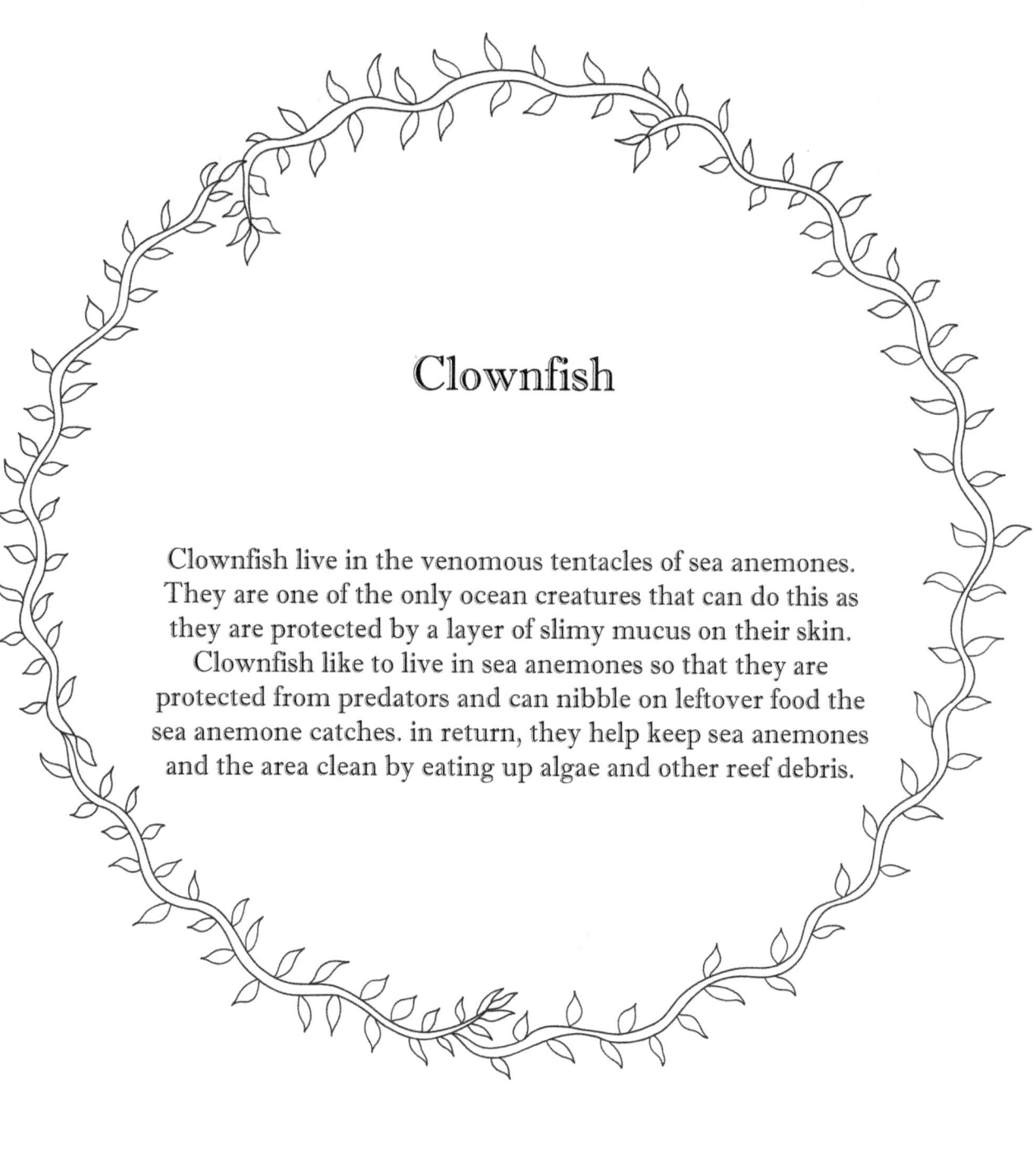

Crab

The crab is a type of crustacean similar to prawns, shrimp and lobster. There are more than 6,700 know species of crabs found in waters worldwide and these many crab species are split into around 93 different crab groups. Most crabs species are found in the shallower ocean waters where the crabs tend to inhabit rocky pools and coral reefs. Crabs typically walk sideways however, some crabs walk forwards or backwards.

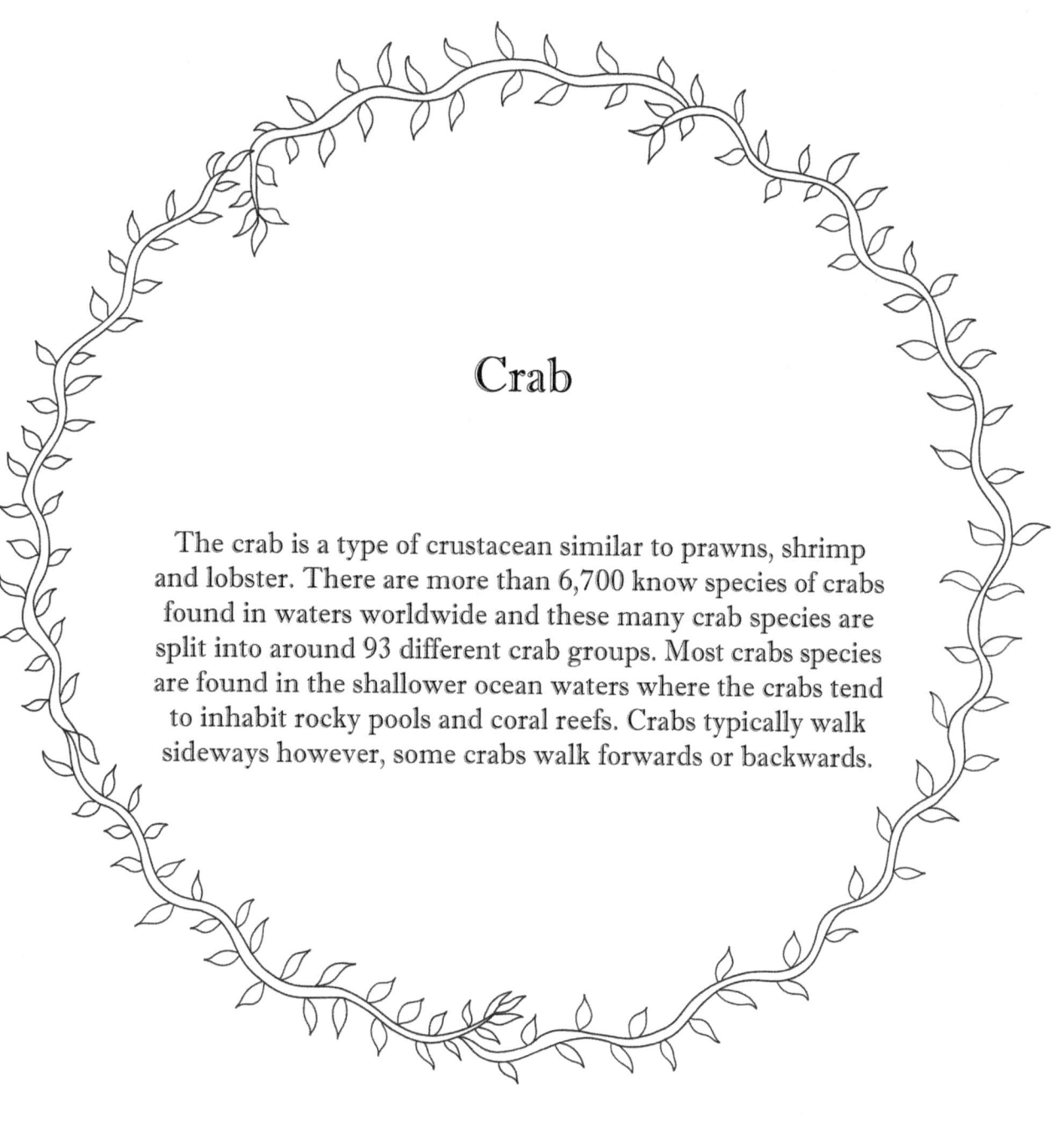

Lightning Whelk Shell

The lighting whelk (Busycon contrarium) is a marine gastropod mollusk, which basically means that it is a sea-dwelling snail. This particular species acquired the name "lightning whelk" because the white shells of the juveniles have chestnut brown stripes with a zig-zag pattern reminiscent of lightning bolts. Lightning whelks grow to a length of 10-15 inches and are sometimes mistaken for conchs. They live in shallow water and prefer embayments having sandy or muddy bottoms. An adult lighting whelk eats about one clam a month, and it's not very picky about the type.

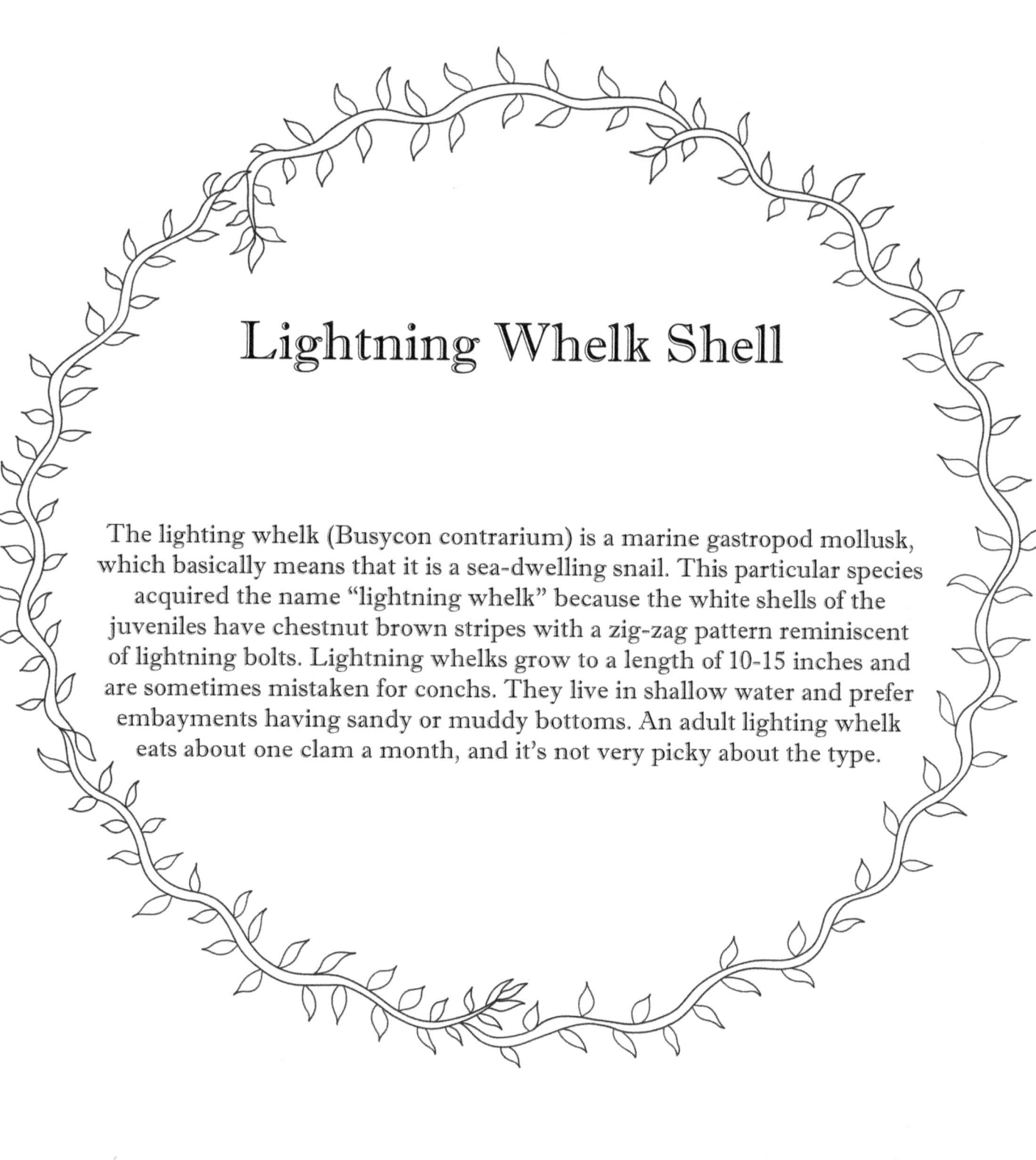

Seahorse

Seahorses are truly unique, and not just because of their unusual equine shape. Unlike most other fish, they are monogamous and mate for life. Rarer still, they are among the only species on Earth in which the male bears the unborn young. Seahorses have no teeth and no stomach, they suck in their food and swallow it whole. Thus their prey needs to be very small. Primarily, seahorses feed on plankton, small fish and small crustaceans, such as shrimp and copepods. Food passes through their digestive systems so quickly they must eat almost constantly to stay alive. Sea horses are found in shallow tropical and temperate waters throughout the world.

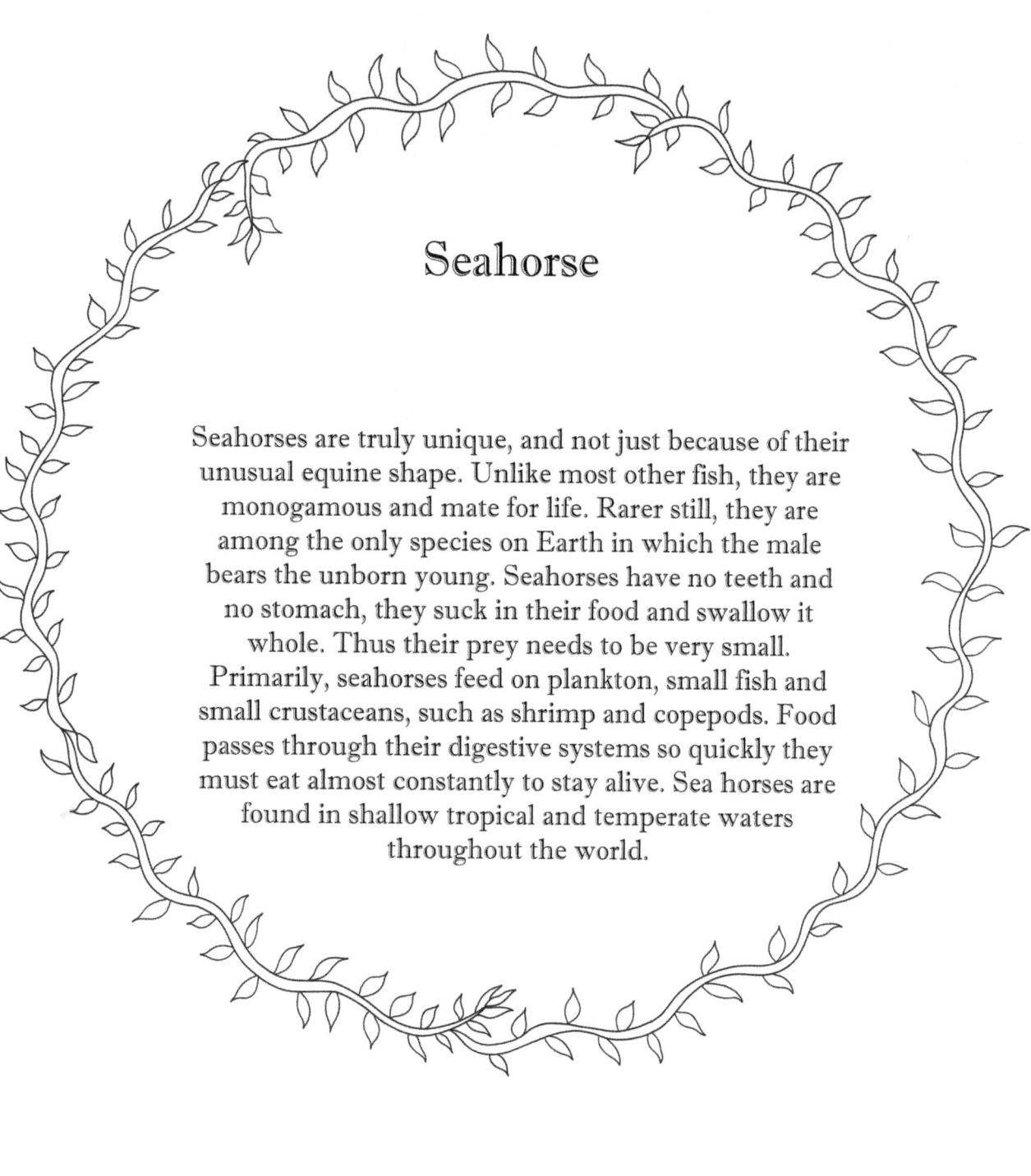

www.ingramcontent.com/pod-product-compliance
Lightning Source LLC
Chambersburg PA
CBHW081015040426
42444CB00014B/3224